Teacher Messages
for Home
in English and Spanish

Grades K-2

By
Katherine L. Ruggieri, M.Ed.

Published by Fearon Teacher Aids
an imprint of

 McGraw Hill Children's Publishing

Author: Katherine L. Ruggieri, M.Ed.
Editors: Kristin Eclov, Michael Batty
Inside Illustrations: Megan Jeffries
Translation: Linguistic Systems, Inc.

 **Children's Publishing**

Published by Fearon Teacher Aids
An imprint of McGraw-Hill Children's Publishing
Copyright © 2001 McGraw-Hill Children's Publishing

Send all inquiries to:
McGraw-Hill Children's Publishing
3195 Wilson Drive NW
Grand Rapids, Michigan 49544

Teachers Messages for Home—grades K–2
ISBN: 0-7682-0651-0

2 3 4 5 6 7 8 9 MAL 08 07 06 05 04

Table of Contents

4

Introduction

About This Book

Communication between teacher and parent is the cornerstone of a successful school experience. You, the teacher, are the link between home and school. Parents need to hear from you if their children's classwork is not meeting standards, if their children's behavior is problematic, if an assignment is incomplete, if a field trip is coming up, if more supplies are needed, if their children are hurt, sick, or upset, if . . . if . . . if. . . .

Keeping parents informed is often a formidable task. However, as the teacher, it is up to you to make sure that each parent is kept adequately apprised of his or her child's progress. Without a selection of pre-prepared forms, you could easily find yourself struggling to compose several notes simultaneously from scratch. An incomplete or unclear message sent home could result in confusion and additional work.

The degree of clear and open communication established with parents will have a direct and profound impact on the success and effectiveness of your school year. The forms in this book will let you get your messages to parents without having to spend time preparing a new form for every occasion. They will also help you to communicate with Spanish-speaking parents. By providing forms that cover most situations, *Teacher Messages for Home* helps make that vital communication between home and school more efficient and more convenient for the teacher.

5

How to Use This Book

Each form in this book can be photocopied in advance and stored in labeled files. This way, the forms will be ready to be pulled out as needed. It may be helpful to make two-sided copies, with the Spanish version on one side and the English on the other.

The use of each form will determine whether it will be needed for individual students (I) or for the whole class (WC), which will give you an idea of how many copies should be kept on hand.

The information needed for the forms can be handwritten or typed in. In some situations, a teacher may want to use a form as a guideline to create a handwritten form for a specific purpose.

To avoid confusion, the term *parent* also refers to legal guardian. In some instances, you may want to substitute the words *legal guardian* for *parent* before sending a form home.

When to Use This Book

Each chapter of *Teacher Messages for Home* contains forms relating to particular needs. The table of contents lists the titles of every form in each chapter. Take the time to thumb through the book to familiarize yourself with the forms. Afterward, you will know when each is appropriate to use.

At the end of the school year, you will reflect on how often you had to send notes to parents and will realize the size of the task. The ready-made forms in *Teacher Messages for Home* will help you achieve and maintain effective communication with parents.

1. Beginning of the Year

Positive, year-long communication between teacher and parents will create the firm foundation that students need to get the most from their school experiences. As the academic year begins, a lot of important information must be sent to parents. This information, presented in a clear and timely manner, will set the expectation for productive communication throughout the year.

Welcome to the _____ Grade

This form presents the daily schedule and lists the general topics to be covered during the year. The list of topics provides an overview of general themes or subjects to be studied; the daily schedule does the same for the students' school day. Items of interest generally include activities that require students to move from one place to another, such as recess, lunch, physical education, or special activities. (WC)

Supply List for _____ Grade

This list provides a way to request basic supplies needed for the year. Be sure to describe specific needs, such as rulers that must be plastic or pencils that must have #2 lead. List supplies in two columns, one for items on which the student's name must be written, and the other for items that do not need a label. (WC)

Classroom Rules

The classroom rules sheet lists desirable qualities for classroom conduct. These rules may be modified later by you and your class, or may be considered a finished product. Copy these lists on 8-1/2" x 11" pages for posting around the classroom or enlarge them onto poster board. (WC)

Student Information

This form lists emergency information and information about the individual child. The interest items will help you get to know your students a little better and often provide ideas for individual projects or assignments. This information can be kept in your classroom, either in individual files or in one folder labeled *Current Student Information*. (WC)

Hopes and Dreams

This form is designed to let parents tell you about their children. As the teacher, it is important for you to be aware of each child's uniqueness. Parents usually welcome the opportunity to share what they believe is special about their children. Requesting this information lets parents know that you are on the same team. Keep this information on file and refer to it throughout the year. (WC)

Classroom Helpers

This form is designed to encourage parents to participate however they can. Parent helpers can be a great resource. You may want to wait until you have established your classroom expectations before inviting parents in. Send this form out when you are ready to have them help you. (WC)

© Fearon Teacher Aids FE11050

Name _____

Welcome to the ____ Grade

Topics about which we will be learning:

_____

_____

_____

_____

Here is our daily schedule:

Time   **Subject**

_____ to _____ , _____

_____ to _____ , _____

_____ to _____ , _____

_____ to _____ , _____

_____ to _____ , _____

_____ to _____ , _____

Nombre_____

Bienvenido/a ___ grado

Temas sobre lo que aprenderemos:

_____

_____

_____

_____

Éste es nuestro horario diario

Hora   **Tema**

_____ a _____ , _____

_____ a _____ , _____

_____ a _____ , _____

_____ a _____ , _____

_____ a _____ , _____

_____ a _____ , _____

Name _____

Supply List for ____ Grade

Dear Parent,

We will have a busy year full of learning. Below is a list of the things your child will need. Some items should be clearly marked with your child's name, but others need not be marked. Please send these articles to school as soon as possible.

Thanks, _____

Labeled items   **Unlabeled**

_____   _____

_____   _____

_____   _____

_____   _____

_____   _____

_____   _____

_____   _____

Lista de materiales para ____ grado

Estimados Padres/ Encargados:

Tendremos un año con numerosas actividades y aprenderemos mucho. A continuación se incluye una lista de las cosas que necesitará su niño/a. Algunas de ellas deberán estar claramente rotuladas con el nombre de su niño/a. Para otras la marcación no será necesario. Por favor, envíe estos artículos a la escuela lo antes posible.

Muchas gracias, _____

Artículos rotulados

_____

_____

_____

_____

_____

_____

No rotulados

_____

_____

_____

_____

_____

_____

 Name_____

Classroom Rules

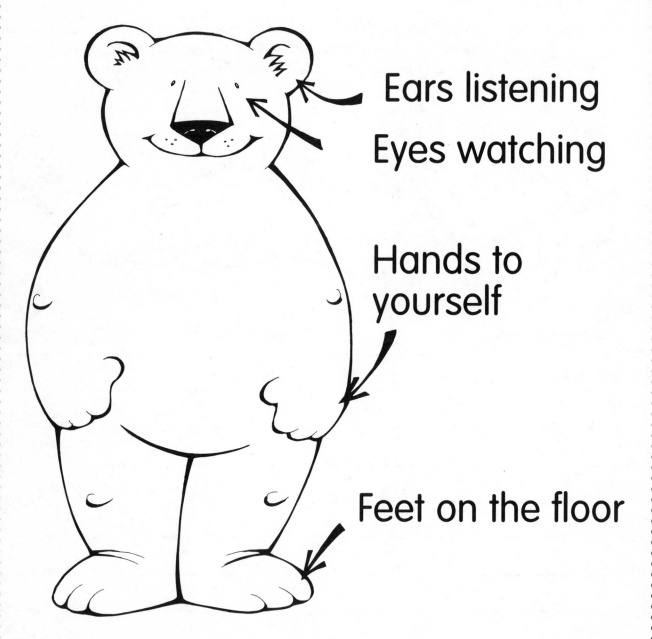

Ears listening

Eyes watching

Hands to yourself

Feet on the floor

Nombre

Las reglas de la clase

Los oídos escuchan

Los ojos miran

Las manos contigo

Los pies en el piso

reproducible

13

© Fearon Teacher Aids FE11050

 Name _____

In Our Class

Be a helper.

Listen.

Be kind.

Work quietly.

 Nombre _____

En nuestra clase

Ayuda.

Escucha.

Sé amable.

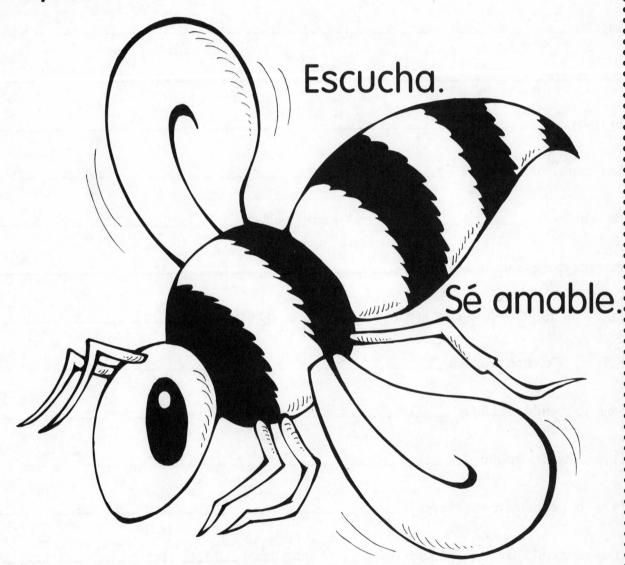

Trabaja en silencio.

reproducible   15   © Fearon Teacher Aids FE11050

Student Information

Please help me get to know your child better.

Name: _____ Nickname (if any): _____

Address: _____

_____

Birthday: _____

Family members at home: _____

Favorite food: _____ Favorite hobby: _____

Favorite thing to do as a family: _____

Does your child watch television daily? _____ How much? _____

Favorite television program: _____

Does your child read daily? _____ How much? _____

Favorite type of reading: _____

Does your child have any allergies? _____

Does your child have any special restrictions or limitations? _____

_____

Please add any other information that you think would be helpful. _____

_____

Información del/de la alumno/a

Por favor, ayúdeme a conocer mejor a su niño/a.

Nombre: _____ Sobrenombre (si tiene): _____

Dirección: _____

_____

Cumpleaños: _____

Miembros de la familia que viven en la casa: _____

Comida preferida:_____ Pasatiempo favorito:_____

Lo que más le gusta hacer con su familia:_____

¿Mira la televisión diariamente su niño/a? _____ ¿Cuántas horas? _____

Programa de televisión favorito: _____

¿Lee diariamente su niño/a?_____ ¿Cuánto?_____

Tipo de lectura preferida:_____

¿Tiene alergiás su niño/a? _____

¿Tiene su niño/a alguna restricción o limitación especial? _____

_____

Por favor, agregue otra información que Ud. crea pueda sernos útil._____

_____

Hopes and Dreams

Date: _____

Dear Parents:

It is very important for me to know your hopes and dreams for your child this year.
I know what a treasure your children are to you.

Please tell me the special things you see in _____
that you would like me to see, too. (Please attach another sheet of paper if necessary.)

_____

_____

_____

_____

_____

_____

_____

_____

_____

_____

_____

Please return this form as soon as possible.
Thank you,

_____

Sueños y esperanzas

Fecha:_____

Estimados Padres/ Encargados:

Es muy importante para mí conocer sus sueños y esperanzas para su niño/a para este año. Sé que sus niños son un tesoro para Ustedes.

Por favor, díganme qué cosas especiales ven en _____ que quisieran que yo también viera. (Sírvanse agregar otra hoja si es necesario.)

_____

_____

_____

_____

_____

_____

_____

_____

_____

_____

_____

_____

Por favor, devuelvan este formulario tan pronto como les sea posible.

Muchas gracias,

_____

Classroom Helpers

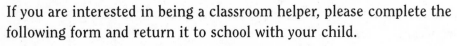

Classroom helpers are an important part of our classroom. Helpers can participate in many ways, such as preparing materials, working with students individually or in small groups, correcting papers, and accompanying us on field trips.

If you are interested in being a classroom helper, please complete the following form and return it to school with your child.

☐ I would like to be a weekly helper.

Best day of the week: _____ Best time of the day: _____

Area(s) in which I would like to help: _____

Special talents I have: _____

☐ I would like to be a monthly helper.

Best day of the month: _____ Best time of the day: _____

Area(s) in which I would like to help: _____

Special talents I have: _____

☐ I would like to help on field trips. ☐ I would like to help with class parties.

☐ I would like to help by doing work at home and returning it to school with my child.

Area(s) in which I would like to help: _____

Special talents I have: _____

Signature: _____

Telephone number and best time to call: _____

Ayudantes de clase

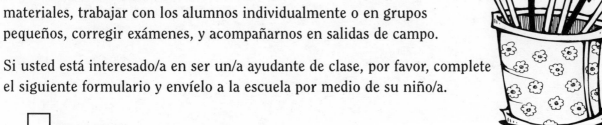

Los ayudantes de clase son una parte importante de nuestra clase. Los ayudantes pueden participar de muchas maneras, como preparar materiales, trabajar con los alumnos individualmente o en grupos pequeños, corregir exámenes, y acompañarnos en salidas de campo.

Si usted está interesado/a en ser un/a ayudante de clase, por favor, complete el siguiente formulario y envíelo a la escuela por medio de su niño/a.

☐ Me gustaría ser un ayudante semanal.

Mejor día de la semana: _____ Mejor momento del día: _____

Área/s en la/s que me gustaría ayudar: _____

Talentos especiales que poseo: _____

☐ Me gustaría ser un ayudante mensual.

Mejor día del mes: _____ Mejor momento del día: _____

Área/s en la/s que me gustaría ayudar: _____

Talentos especiales que poseo: _____

☐ Me gustaría ayudar en salidas de campo. ☐ Me gustaría ayudar con las fiestas de la clase.

☐ Me gustaría ayudar haciendo tareas en casa y devolviéndolas a la escuela por medio de mi niño/a.

Áreas en las que me gustaría ayudar: _____

Talentos especiales que poseo: _____

Firma: _____

Número telefónico y mejor horario para llamar: _____

2. Homework and Study Habits

Homework is an important part of the school experience, and parents, teachers, and students need to work together to ensure that it gets done. The forms in this section help parents understand what is required of their children and how their children are performing. Because young students sometimes forget why they have taken an assignment home and don't remember when it is due, these forms keep students and parents informed. Some forms require a parent signature.

Homework Calendar

This calendar provides a clear and simple way for students to keep track of homework assignments and accomplishments for the entire week. Each day, assignments are written on the forms and students take

them home for their parents to see. Parents sign the forms and send them back to school. This procedure is repeated each day of the week. A reward system can be used for students who get parent signatures each day of the week. (WC)

My Weekly Homework Report

This form allows quick feedback on a daily basis. It is intended to be sent home at the end of each day after the teacher has looked over the day's homework. If work needs to be redone, it can be stapled to the report. Checkmarks can be used to indicate that the homework is finished and correct. A percentage could be written to evaluate the student's homework performance. (WC)

Oops! I Forgot!

This is just a quick reminder to be used for forgotten schoolwork or other items. Copy onto brightly colored paper to make it more noticeable. (WC)

Work Slip

This can be attached to work that was not finished in class and that needs to be taken home. It tells the parents exactly what should be done and when it should be returned to school. (WC)

My Daily Report

This form is a daily behavior record. Acknowledgment of good behavior can help students working to modify their behavior. It informs parents in a nonthreatening way how their child is doing on a daily basis. These forms can be returned to school to be filed or left at home with the parents. If the form is to be left at home, make a copy. (WC)

Sorry You're Sick

Use this to tell students what assignments they have missed while sick. It can be sent home daily with work so that the student doesn't get too far behind. If work is not picked up daily, list the assignments on the slips. That way, you won't have to search for what was done on each day of a child's absence. (WC)

Name _____

Homework Calendar

Week of _____

Monday assignment: _____

_____

Parent signature: _____

....

Tuesday assignment: _____

_____

Parent signature: _____

....

Wednesday assignment: _____

_____

Parent signature: _____

....

Thursday assignment: _____

_____

Parent signature: _____

....

Friday assignment: _____

_____

Parent signature: _____

Nombre _____

Calendario de tareas para el hogar

Semana de _____

Tarea para el lunes:_____

_____

Firma del padre/madre/encargado: _____

Tarea para el martes: _____

_____

Firma del padre/madre/encargado: _____

Tarea para el miércoles:_____

_____

Firma del padre/madre/encargado: _____

Tarea para el jueves:_____

_____

Firma del padre/madre/encargado: _____

Tarea para el viernes: _____

_____

Firma del padre/madre/encargado: _____

Name _____

My Weekly Homework Report

Teacher: _____

Week of _____ Room: _____

MONDAY

Homework turned in: ☐YES ☐NO

Homework completely finished: ☐YES ☐NO

Homework correct: ☐YES ☐NO

Try again: ☐YES ☐NO

TUESDAY

Homework turned in: ☐YES ☐NO

Homework completely finished: ☐YES ☐NO

Homework correct: ☐YES ☐NO

Try again: ☐YES ☐NO

WEDNESDAY

Homework turned in: ☐YES ☐NO

Homework completely finished: ☐YES ☐NO

Homework correct: ☐YES ☐NO

Try again: ☐YES ☐NO

THURSDAY

Homework turned in: ☐YES ☐NO

Homework completely finished: ☐YES ☐NO

Homework correct: ☐YES ☐NO

Try again: ☐YES ☐NO

FRIDAY

Homework turned in: ☐YES ☐NO

Homework completely finished: ☐YES ☐NO

Homework correct: ☐YES ☐NO

Try again: ☐YES ☐NO

© Fearon Teacher Aids FE11050

Nombre_____

Mi informe de tareas semanal

Maestra/o: _____

Semana de _____ Aula:_____

LUNES

Tarea entregada: ☐ SÍ ☐ NO

Tarea completamente terminada: ☐ SÍ ☐ NO

Tarea correcta: ☐ SÍ ☐ NO

Nuevo intento: ☐ SÍ ☐ NO

MARTES

Tarea entregada: ☐ SÍ ☐ NO

Tarea completamente terminada: ☐ SÍ ☐ NO

Tarea correcta: ☐ SÍ ☐ NO

Nuevo intento: ☐ SÍ ☐ NO

MIÉRCOLES

Tarea entregada: ☐ SÍ ☐ NO

Tarea completamente terminada: ☐ SÍ ☐ NO

Tarea correcta: ☐ SÍ ☐ NO

Nuevo intento: ☐ SÍ ☐ NO

JUEVES

Tarea entregada: ☐ SÍ ☐ NO

Tarea completamente terminada: ☐ SÍ ☐ NO

Tarea correcta: ☐ SÍ ☐ NO

Nuevo intento: ☐ SÍ ☐ NO

VIERNES

Tarea entregada: ☐ SÍ ☐ NO

Tarea completamente terminada: ☐ SÍ ☐ NO

Tarea correcta: ☐ SÍ ☐ NO

Nuevo intento: ☐ SÍ ☐ NO

Oops! I Forgot!

Date: _____

Your child, _____ ,

forgot to bring his/her _____

to school today.

Please help him/her to remember to bring it tomorrow.

Thank you,

_____

✂ - ✂

Oops! I Forgot!

Date: _____

Your child, _____ ,

forgot to bring his/her _____

to school today.

Please help him/her to remember to bring it tomorrow.

Thank you,

_____

¡Ay! ¡Me Olvidé!

Fecha:_____

Su niño/a, _____ ,

hoy se le olvidó traer su _____

a la escuela.

Por favor, ayúdelo/a a recordar que lo traiga mañana.

Muchas gracias.

_____

✂ - ✂

¡Ay! ¡Me Olvidé!

Fecha:_____

Su niño/a, _____ ,

hoy se le olvidó traer su _____

a la escuela.

Por favor, ayúdelo/a a recordar que lo traiga mañana.

Muchas gracias.

_____

Work Slip

Date: _____

Your child, _____ ,

needs to work on his/her _____

and return it to school tomorrow.

Signed,

_____

 ✂ ----- ✂

Work Slip

Date: _____

Your child, _____ ,

needs to work on his/her _____

and return it to school tomorrow.

Signed,

_____

Hojita de trabajo

Fecha: _____

Su niño/a, _____ ,

necesita trabajar en su _____

y devolverlo a la escuela mañana.

Firmado,

_____

Hojita de trabajo

Fecha: _____

Su niño/a, _____ ,

necesita trabajar en su _____

y devolverlo a la escuela mañana.

Firmado,

_____

Name _____

My Daily Report

Week of _____

Monday	I was a good listener.	I finished my work.	I got along with others.
Tuesday	I was a good listener.	I finished my work.	I got along with others.
Wednesday	I was a good listener.	I finished my work.	I got along with others.
Thursday	I was a good listener.	I finished my work.	I got along with others.
Friday	I was a good listener.	I finished my work.	I got along with others.

...ne diario

Semana de _____

Lunes

Escuché con atención.

Terminé mi trabajo.

Me llevé bien con los demás.

Martes

Escuché con atención.

Terminé mi trabajo.

Me llevé bien con los demás.

Miércoles

Escuché con atención.

Terminé mi trabajo.

Me llevé bien con los demás.

Jueves

Escuché con atención.

Terminé mi trabajo.

Me llevé bien con los demás.

Viernes

Escuché con atención.

Terminé mi trabajo.

Me llevé bien con los demás.

Sorry you're sick. Please get well soon. We miss you!

Work for _____ Date: _____

Writing _____

Math _____

Reading _____

Spelling _____

Social studies/science _____

Special information _____

✂ — ✂

Sorry you're sick. Please get well soon. We miss you!

Work for _____ Date: _____

Writing _____

Math _____

Reading _____

Spelling _____

Social studies/science _____

Special information _____

¡Qué pena que estés enfermo/a! Ojalá te mejores pronto.
¡Te extrañamos!

Tarea para el día _____ Fecha: _____

Escritura _____

Matemáticas _____

Lectura _____

Ortografía _____

Estudios Sociales/Ciencias _____

Información especial _____

✂ - ✂

¡Qué pena que estés enfermo/a! Ojalá te mejores pronto.
¡Te extrañamos!

Tarea para el día _____ Fecha: _____

Escritura _____

Matemáticas _____

Lectura _____

Ortografía _____

Estudios Sociales/Ciencias _____

Información especial _____

3. Organizational Tools and Calendars

A student whose work habits are well organized has a good chance of having a productive and satisfactory school experience. The basic tools of organization can be taught to students at any age. Knowing these enables both the child and his or her parents to keep track of the numerous activities of a school day.

Monthly Calendar

This calendar template serves a twofold purpose: it can be used for practice filling in months and dates or for scheduling assignments. Tell the students which activities or assignments go on which dates, and they can complete the calendar in class. The calendar can include assignment due dates, field trips, long-term projects, and other items. (WC)

What Did I Do Today?

This form addresses the age-old question that parents like to ask and students seldom know how to answer: "What did you do today?" Space is provided for students to make daily notes of three or four things they did in school on each day of the week. Entries might include *math—adding, science—magnets, language—nouns, and art—paint*. Check the students' papers before they leave. A smiley face or star can indicate that you have seen the paper and consider it ready to go home. A weekly reward will encourage students to keep track of their papers and to take them home and bring them back to school each day. (WC)

My Weekly Goal

This is a basic goal sheet for students to complete at school and take home for parents to review. It can be completed on Monday as a class activity. Write suggestions on the board for students to copy onto their goal sheets. Goals should be as specific as possible and written in child-friendly language. Goals might include the following: *get my work finished, write my spelling words 5 times every night, read for 15 minutes each night*, and *make my Rs the right way*. (WC)

Classroom News

This template gives you an opportunity to communicate with the parents about what has happened in the classroom during a given week. The form can be filled out daily or at the end of the week and sent home with students on Fridays. Notes can be added to remind parents about upcoming events or assignments or to thank them for help on field trips or class activities. Weekly communication helps parents feel involved and informed. When you use this form, consistency is important. Parents will become accustomed to seeing it on Fridays. (WC)

Name _____

Monthly Calendar

Calendar for the month of _____

Sunday	Monday	Tuesday	Wednesday	Thursday	Friday	Saturday

reproducible

Nombre _____

✏ Calendario Mensual

Calendario para el m es de _____

Domingo	Lunes	Martes	Miércoles	Jueves	Viernes	Sábado

reproducible

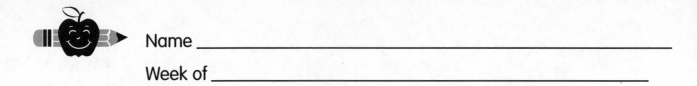

Name _____

Week of _____

What Did I Do Today?

Monday _____

_____

Parent signature: _____

· ·

Tuesday _____

_____

Parent signature: _____

· ·

Wednesday _____

_____

Parent signature: _____

· ·

Thursday _____

_____

Parent signature: _____

· ·

Friday _____

_____

Parent signature: _____

· ·

Nombre_____

Semana de_____

 ¿Qué hice hoy?

Lunes
_____

_____

Firma del padre/ madre/ encargado:_____

Martes
_____

_____

Firma del padre/ madre/ encargado:_____

Miércoles
_____

_____

Firma del padre/ madre/ encargado:_____

Jueves
_____

_____

Firma del padre/ madre/ encargado:_____

Viernes
_____

_____

Firma del padre/ madre/ encargado:_____

 Name _____

My Weekly Goal

Date: _____

Dear _____,

This week in school my goal is
_____
_____
_____
_____
_____
_____
_____ .

Please help me accomplish my goal. Thank you.

Signed, _____

 Nombre _____

Fecha: _____

Querido _____ ,

Esta semana en la escuela mi meta es
_____
_____
_____
_____
_____
_____
_____ .

Por favor ayúdeme a lograr mi objetivo. Muchas gracias.

Firmado, _____

Classroom News

Week of _____

Teacher: _____ Room: _____

Monday	Tuesday
Wednesday	Thursday
Friday	Notes

Noticias de clase

Semana de_____

Maestro/a:_____ Aula: _____

Lunes	Martes
Miércoles	Jueves
Viernes	Notas

4. School Events

During the school year there will be many opportunities for parents to be involved in school activities. For children, sharing their school, their classroom, and their work with their parents can be a positive experience. Let parents know about school activities or events as far in advance as you can.

Event Calendar

This calendar provides space to highlight events during a given month and gives parents the chance to plan ahead. Write the time each activity begins and ends so parents know how much time is involved. (WC)

Join Us!

This is an invitation to parents to come to the classroom for a special event, such as a presentation of reports, an art activity, a play or skit, or a special guest speaker. Let parents know exactly when the event will start and how long it will last so they can make the necessary arrangements. (WC)

Open House

This invitation tells parents that you are looking forward to seeing them in your classroom. It lets them know when your classroom will be open and what will be featured in your room. (WC)

Helpers Needed

Many events require parent help. This request lets parents know what is planned and what type of help is needed. (WC)

Thank You

Thank-you notes are an important part of your communication with parents. The notes let parents know how much you appreciate them. Students can add handwritten notes. (WC)

Event Calendar

Name _____

For the month of _____

Sunday	Monday	Tuesday	Wednesday	Thursday	Friday	Saturday

reproducible

Nombre _____

Calendario de acontecimientos

Para el mes de _____

Domingo	Lunes	Martes	Miércoles	Jueves	Viernes	Sábado

Join Us!

Please come to our classroom on _____ .

We will be

_____

_____

_____ .

Please join us from _____ to _____ .

Hope to see you there!

¡Visítenos!

Por favor, venga a nuestra clase el día _____ .

Nosotros

_____

_____

_____ .

Por favor, visítenos de _____ a _____ .

¡Esperamos verlo/a allí!

Open House

Date: _____

Please come visit our classroom and see what's new.

Our room, _____, will be open from _____ to _____ .

We have been working hard and want to show you our

_____

_____

_____ .

Please
join us.

Casa abierta

Fecha: _____

Venga a visitar nuestra clase y vea qué hay de nuevo.

Nuestra aula, _____, estará abierta de _____ a _____.

Hemos trabajado con esmero y queremos mostrarle nuestro/a

_____

_____

_____.

¡Lo/a esperamos!

Helpers Needed

Our school is having a _____

on _____ .

We're doing this to _____

_____ .

We would like to have help.

We need people to _____

_____ .

Please let me know if you would like to help.

Thank you.

Signed,

_____

Se necesitan ayudantes

Nuestra escuela va a _____
el día _____ .

Esto, lo hacemos para_____
_____ .

Nos gustaría que nos ayudaran.

Necesitamos gente para_____
_____ .

Por favor, avíseme si le gustaría ayudar.

Gracias.

Firmado,

_____

Thank You!

Dear _____ ,

Thank you for helping out!
We couldn't have done it without you!

From all of us in Room _____

 ✂ - ✂

Thank You!

Dear _____ ,

Thank you for helping out!
We couldn't have done it without you!

From all of us in Room _____

...cias!

Estimado/a _____,

¡Gracias por ayudarnos!
¡No podríamos haberlo hecho sin usted!

Por parte de todas nosotros
en el Aula _____

✂ - ✂

¡Gracias!

Estimado/a _____,

¡Gracias por ayudarnos!
¡No podríamos haberlo hecho sin usted!

Por parte de todas nosotros
en el Aula_____

5. Field Trips

Field trips can be a great part of the school experience. They offer opportunities to take learning beyond the school site. Field trips must be thoroughly planned well in advance to be sure that things go smoothly. As soon as your field trip is scheduled, let parents know.

Field Trip Announcement

This informs parents about upcoming field trips. It lets them know when, where, and why. Space is provided on the same form to let parents know if they are needed to help. (WC)

Field Trip Reminder

This reminds parents and students about the upcoming field trip. It reminds them when it is, where they will be going, and what their children need to bring. Send this out two or three days before the field trip. (WC)

Field Trip Volunteers

This form lets you inform parents whether or not you need them to help. Often you will have too many volunteers and will want to let some of them know that they are not needed this time. (WC)

Field Trip Helpers

Once parent helpers have been chosen, this form can be used to give them more specific instructions and the names of the children they will be supervising. Instructions can be tailored to fit each field trip. Parents should keep these forms with them during the trip. (WC)

Thank You

After the trip, be sure to let parents know how much you appreciate their help by sending a thank-you note. Everyone likes to feel appreciated. Students can add handwritten notes. (WC)

Field Trip Announcement

Dear Parent,

Our class will be going on a field trip on _____.

We will go to _____

_____.

We are going in order to _____

_____.

We will go by _____ and will leave from _____

at _____.

We will go back to _____ at _____.

Parent Helpers

☐ Adult helpers are needed. Please send a note if you would like to help.

☐ Adult helpers are not needed at this time.

Supervision will be provided by_____.

Thank you.

Signed,

_____

Anuncio de salida de campo

Estimado padre/ madre/ encargado:

Nuestra clase hará una salida de campo el día _____ .

Iremos a _____

_____ .

Vamos a ir para _____

_____ .

Iremos en _____ y partiremos de _____

a las _____ .

Regresaremos a _____ a las _____ .

Padres ayudantes

☐ Se necesitan adultos ayudantes. Por favor, envíenos una nota si le gustaría ayudar.

☐ Esta vez no se necesitan adultos ayudantes.

La supervisión estará a cargo de _____ .

Gracias.

Firmado,

_____

Field Trip Reminder

The big day is coming!

On _____ we will go to _____ .

We are leaving from _____ at _____ .

Don't forget to bring the following:

_____

_____

_____

We're in for a great time!
Please be prompt!

Recordatorio de salida de campo

¡Se acerca
el gran día!

El día _____ iremos a _____.

Salimos de _____ a las _____.

¡Que no se les olvide traer lo siguiente!

_____

_____

_____

¡Esperamos disfrutarlo mucho!
¡Por favor, vengan a buena hora!

Field Trip Volunteers

Dear Parent,

Thank you for volunteering to help on our field trip to _____

on_____.

☐ We have plenty of help this time. May we call if someone cancels?

☐ We need help supervising a group of children. Please arrive at school by _____.

Thanks for your support.

✂ - ✂

Field Trip Volunteers

Dear Parent,

Thank you for volunteering to help on our field trip to _____

on_____.

☐ We have plenty of help this time. May we call if someone cancels?

☐ We need help supervising a group of children. Please arrive at school by _____.

Thanks for your support.

Voluntarios para salida de campo

Estimado padre/ madre/ encargado:

Gracias por ofrecerse a ayudarnos en nuestra salida de campo a ——————

el día ————————————————————————————————————— .

☐ Esta vez tenemos muchos ofrecimientos de ayuda. ¿Podemos llamarlo si alguien cancela?

☐ Necesitamos ayuda para supervisar a un grupo de niños. Por favor llegue a
la escuela antes de las ————— .

Gracias por su apoyo.

✂ - ✂

Voluntarios para salida de campo

Estimado padre/ madre/ encargado:

Gracias por ofrecerse a ayudarnos en nuestra salida de campo a ——————

el día ————————————————————————————————————— .

☐ Esta vez tenemos muchos ofrecimientos de ayuda. ¿Podemos llamarlo si alguien cancela?

☐ Necesitamos ayuda para supervisar a un grupo de niños. Por favor llegue a
la escuela antes de las ————— .

Gracias por su apoyo.

© Fearon Teacher Aids FE11050

Field Trip Helpers

Thank you for helping.
Your group of children includes the following:

_____

_____

_____

Keep these children with you at all times. Remind them to use their best behavior.
Other specific instructions:

_____

_____

Sincerely, _____

Field Trip Helpers

Thank you for helping.
Your group of children includes the following:

_____

_____

_____

Keep these children with you at all times. Remind them to use their best behavior.
Other specific instructions:

_____

_____

Sincerely, _____

Ayudantes de la salida de campo

Gracias por ayudarnos.
El grupo de niños que irá con usted incluye a los siguientes:

_____

_____

_____

Mantenga a estos niños con usted en todo momento. Recuérdeles que se comporten de la mejor manera.
Otras instrucciones específicas.

_____

_____

Cordialmente, _____

✂ --- ✂

Ayudantes de la salida de campo

Gracias por ayudarnos.
El grupo de niños que irá con usted incluye a los siguientes:

_____

_____

_____

Mantenga a estos niños con usted en todo momento. Recuérdeles que se comporten de la mejor manera.
Otras instrucciones específicas.

_____

_____

Cordialmente, _____

Thank You!

Dear _____,

Thank you for helping on our field trip!
We couldn't have done it without you!

From all of us in Room _____

 -

Thank You!

Dear _____,

Thank you for helping on our field trip!
We couldn't have done it without you!

From all of us in Room _____

¡Gracias!

Estimado/a _____,

¡Gracias por ayudarnos!
¡No podríamos haberlo hecho sin usted!

Por parte de todos nosotros en el Aula _____

¡Gracias!

Estimado/a _____,

¡Gracias por ayudarnos!
¡No podríamos haberlo hecho sin usted!

Por parte de todos nosotros en el Aula _____

70

6. Behavior Issues

During the school year it may become necessary for you to discuss a child's behavior with his or her parents. Such issues should be dealt with as soon as they arise. The student should be aware of the choices that he or she made and of how these have affected others. Helping the student recognize that he or she has choices is a big step in solving behavior issues. Your goal, for the parents, is to inform them of the situation in question, and to bring them on board in an effort to improve the student's behavior. It is important to share positive as well as negative information with parents. Every parent likes to hear the good things that his or her child does.

Making Better Choices

This form presents a step-by-step process with which students may evaluate possible choices. It gives an opportunity for them to review what happened, what they did, how they felt, and what they might try next time. Students should fill this out with the help of the teacher. (I)

I Always Have a Choice

This visual organizer helps students think about and write down good choices. It can be done independently or with adult supervision. It can be kept on file for the student to review when necessary. (WC)

I'm Proud of Myself

These notes are to be taken home and shared with parents. The messages encourage communication between parents and students regarding good things that occur at school. Students can select notes, or the teacher can pass them out when appropriate. (WC)

Great Behavior

This note is used to celebrate great behavior. When a student does something "great," this is a quick way to celebrate. This note can be filled out by the teacher or by other students, depending on their ages. If a student fills it out, be sure to check and sign it before sending it home. After being sent home for parents to read, these notes can be collected and accumulated for class points or other rewards. (WC)

Good Job!

This letter is a nice way to inform parents of a student's good behavior. When communicating behavior to parents, it is important to share the positive as well as the negative. Use this letter to share good news. (WC)

 # Making Better Choices

My name is _____.

Date: _____

Today I am working on making better choices.

What happened: _____

_____

_____.

What I did: _____

_____

_____.

Why I did it: _____

_____

_____.

How I felt:

☐ Mad   ☐ Frustrated   ☐ Anxious

☐ Lonely   ☐ Confused   ☐ Hurt

Next time I will try to _____

_____

_____.

Signed: _____   Approved: _____

 # Escoger mejor

Mi nombre es _____.

Fecha: _____

Hoy estoy tratando de aprender a escoger mejor.

Qué sucedió: _____
_____
_____.

Qué hice: _____
_____
_____.

Por qué lo hice: _____
_____
_____.

Cómo me sentí:

☐ furioso/a ☐ frustrado/a ☐ ansioso/a

☐ solo/a ☐ confundido/a ☐ lastimado/a

La próxima vez trataré de _____
_____
_____.

Firmado: _____ Aprobado: _____

Name _____

I Always Have a Choice

Choice 1

Choice 2

Choice 3

Siempre tengo opción

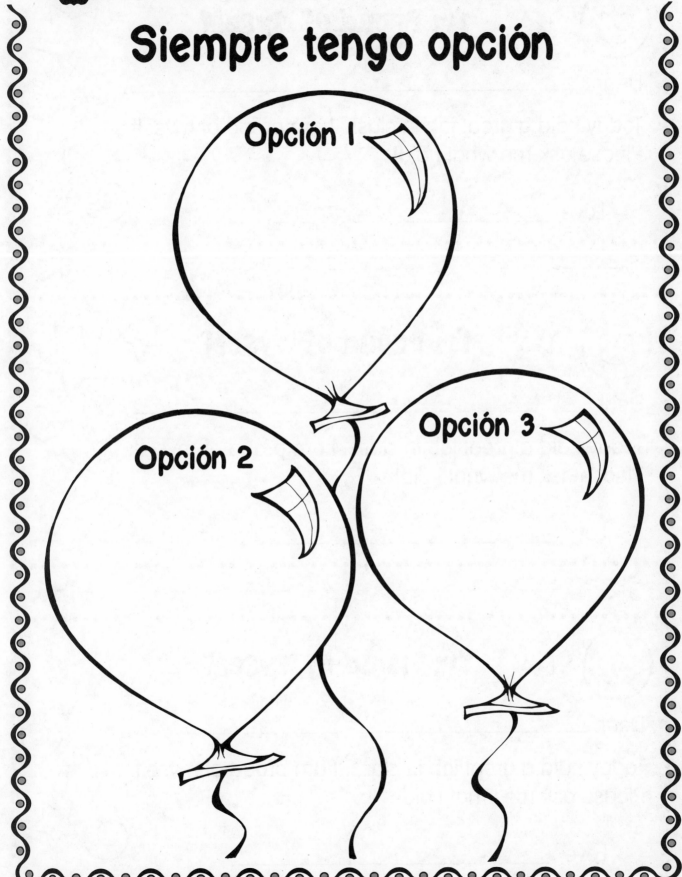

Opción 1

Opción 2

Opción 3

75

© Fearon Teacher Aids FE11050

I'm Proud of Myself

Dear _____,

Today I did a great job in class. I am proud of myself.
Please ask me what I did!

Love, _____

✂ -- ✂

I'm Proud of Myself

Dear _____,

Today I did a great job in class. I am proud of myself.
Please ask me what I did!

Love, _____

✂ -- ✂

I'm Proud of Myself

Dear _____,

Today I did a great job in class. I am proud of myself.
Please ask me what I did!

Love, _____

Estoy orgulloso/a de mí mismo/a

Querido/a _____,

Hoy hice un excelente trabajo en clase.
Estoy orgulloso de mí mismo/a.
Por favor, pregúnteme lo que hice.

Con amor,_____

✂ - ✂

Estoy orgulloso/a de mí mismo/a

Querido/a _____,

Hoy hice un excelente trabajo en clase.
Estoy orgulloso de mí mismo/a.
Por favor, pregúnteme lo que hice.

Con amor,_____

✂ - ✂

Estoy orgulloso/a de mí mismo/a

Querido/a _____,

Hoy hice un excelente trabajo en clase.
Estoy orgulloso de mí mismo/a.
Por favor, pregúnteme lo que hice.

Con amor,_____

© Fearon Teacher Aids FE11050

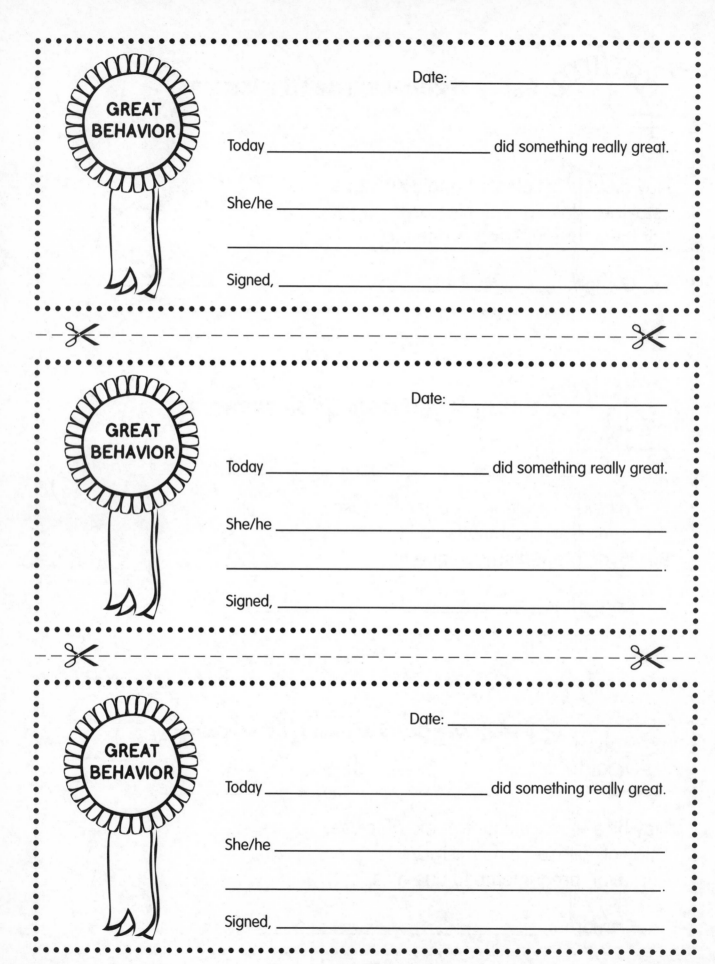

GREAT BEHAVIOR

Date: _____

Today _____ did something really great.

She/he _____

_____.

Signed, _____

✂ - ✂ - - -

GREAT BEHAVIOR

Date: _____

Today _____ did something really great.

She/he _____

_____.

Signed, _____

✂ - ✂ - - -

GREAT BEHAVIOR

Date: _____

Today _____ did something really great.

She/he _____

_____.

Signed, _____

reproducible

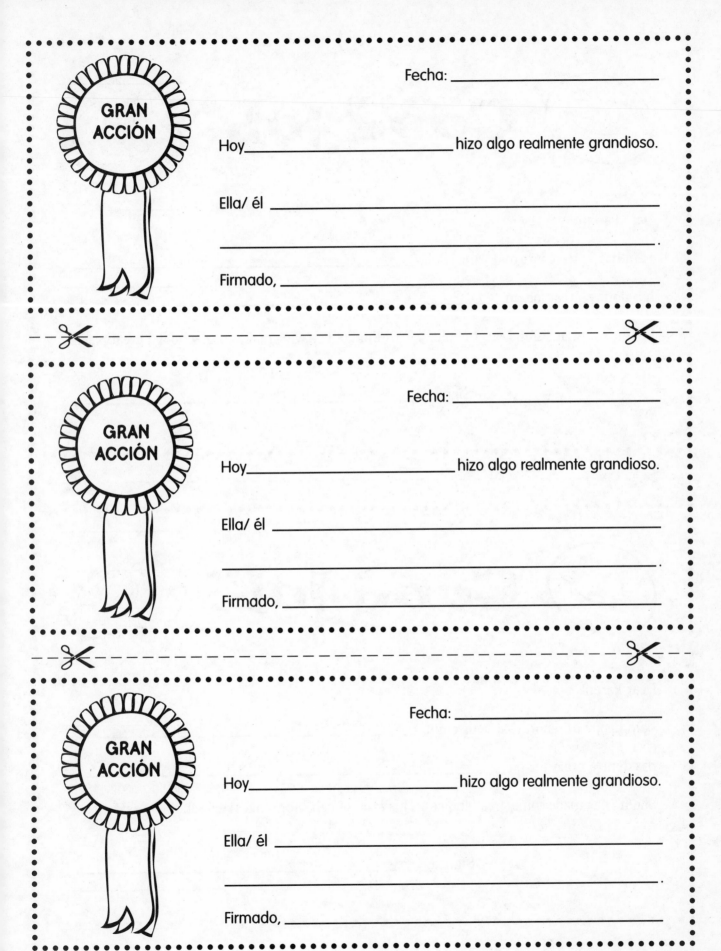

GRAN ACCIÓN

Fecha: _____

Hoy _____ hizo algo realmente grandioso.

Ella/ él _____

_____ .

Firmado, _____

✂- ✂

GRAN ACCIÓN

Fecha: _____

Hoy _____ hizo algo realmente grandioso.

Ella/ él _____

_____ .

Firmado, _____

✂- ✂

GRAN ACCIÓN

Fecha: _____

Hoy _____ hizo algo realmente grandioso.

Ella/ él _____

_____ .

Firmado, _____

 # Good Job!

Dear Parent,

I am happy to report that your child, _____,

has done a great job on _____.

She/he has made some great choices. This kind of behavior makes our school a great place.

Signed, _____

 ✂ — — — — — — — — — — — — — — — — — — ✂ — — —

 # Good Job!

Dear Parent,

I am happy to report that your child, _____,

has done a great job on _____.

She/he has made some great choices. This kind of behavior makes our school a great place.

Signed, _____

reproducible

¡Buen trabajo!

Estimado padre/ madre/ encargado:

Me alegra anunciarle que su niño/a, _____,

hizo un gran trabajo en _____.

Ella/ él eligió muy bien. Este tipo de comportamiento hace de nuestra escuela un lugar maravilloso.

Firmado, _____

¡Buen trabajo!

Estimado padre/ madre/ encargado:

Me alegra anunciarle que su niño/a, _____,

hizo un gran trabajo en _____.

Ella/ él eligió muy bien. Este tipo de comportamiento hace de nuestra escuela un lugar maravilloso.

Firmado, _____

7. Conferences and Conversations

It is often necessary to discuss an issue with a parent. This may regard a school accomplishment or behavior that needs change. Either way, make all communication with parents as positive as possible. When dealing with a student's inappropriate behavior, focus on the solution rather than belaboring the details of the problem. A note may often be sent home, but sometimes it may be necessary to have the parent come in for a talk.

Note Home

This note informs parents about a choice that their child has made at school. Several options may be checked, letting the parent know what the next step should be. (I)

Parent Update

This note provides an update on school behavior. It may address recurring behavior or a first-time event. Space is provided to detail what has occurred. This allows the parent to get a clear picture of what is going on. There are several options at the bottom of the form that can be selected for follow-up. (I)

Reply to Parent

This form is sent in reply to a parent's expressed concerns. It lets the parent know that you have received his or her call or note and describes the action you have taken. When you receive information or inquiries from parents, your reply is vital. (I)

Good News

This is a note to send home to share some great news. It can be given for a kind act, success in a certain subject, or any action that merits a compliment.

It is important to share good news with parents as well as not-so-good news. (WC)

My Accomplishments

This form tells parents what has been going on in class and gives students an opportunity to write about what they have enjoyed. The form can be filled out by students with your guidance and then taken home to be shared with parents. Make copies if you want to keep these in the students' files or yearly portfolios. (WC)

Stop By or Call Me!

This is a quick, whimsical way to let parents know that you have something fun to tell them. You may have a special success to report or an anecdote about their children. (WC)

© Fearon Teacher Aids FE11050

Note Home

Date: _____

Dear _____ ,

This note is to keep you informed about _____ 's

behavior at school. On _____ ,

the following situation occurred:

_____

_____

_____

_____

_____

_____ .

☐ Please discuss this with your child.

☐ Please let me know what you would like to do about this situation.

☐ Please call; I'd like to hear your ideas about this situation.

☐ Please come in and discuss this with me at your earliest convenience.

☐ Please make an appointment to come in and discuss this.

Thank you.

Signed,

_____

Nota para el hogar

Fecha: _____

Estimado/a _____ ,

El objeto de esta nota es mantenerlo/a informado/a acerca del
comportamiento de _____ en la escuela.

El día _____ ,

ocurrió lo siguiente:

_____

_____

_____

_____

_____

_____ .

☐ Por favor, hable de esto con su niño/a.

☐ Por favor, hágame saber qué quisiera hacer al respecto.

☐ Por favor, llámeme. Me gustaría saber qué piensa acerca de esta situación.

☐ Por favor, venga y hable de esto conmigo tan pronto como le sea conveniente.

☐ Por favor, acuerde una cita para venir y tratar el tema.

Muchas gracias.

Firmado,

_____

Parent
U P D A T E

Date: _____

Dear _____,

Today at school _____ made some choices that I would like you to know about.

The incident occurred in/on _____ and involved

_____.

☐ Please discuss this with your child.

☐ Please give me a call at _____.

☐ Please call _____to make an appointment to come in and

discuss this with _____.

Thank you for your support in this.

Sincerely,

_____

Padres/Encargado

N O V E D A D E S

Fecha del día:_____

Estimado/a _____,

Hoy en la escuela _____ hizo algo que me gustaría que usted supiera.

El incidente ocurrió en _____ e involucró

_____ .

☐ Por favor hable de esto con su niño/a.

☐ Por favor llámeme al _____ .

☐ Por favor llame a _____para concretar una cita para venir y tratar el

tema con _____ .

Gracias por su apoyo en esto.

Cordialmente,

_____

Reply to Parent

Date: _____

Dear _____ ,

Thanks for asking/telling me about

_____

_____

_____

_____ .

☐ I appreciate hearing from you, and this is what I have done: _____

_____

☐ I have talked to _____ and worked out the problem.

☐ I have set up an appointment with _____ to discuss this issue.

☐ I have discussed this issue with _____ and made plans to

_____ .

I am requesting more information from _____ .

Please let me know if you have further concerns.

Sincerely,

_____

Respuesta a los padres

Fecha del día: _____

Estimado/a _____,

Gracias por consultarme/ avisarme acerca de

_____

_____

_____

_____ .

☐ Le agradezco habérmelo comunicado, y esto es lo que hice. _____

_____

☐ Hablé con _____ y analizamos la situación.

☐ Acordé una cita con_____ para tratar este tema.

☐ Traté este tema con_____ e hicimos planes para

_____ .

Solicité más información a_____.

Por favor, hágame saber si algo más le preocupa.

Cordialmente,

_____

Super Good News! Wow!

This note is good news about _____.

Today he/she deserves a great big hug for _____

_____.

Hurray for the good things happening at school!

Sincerely, _____

Super Good News! Wow!

This note is good news about _____.

Today he/she deserves a great big hug for _____

_____.

Hurray for the good things happening at school!

Sincerely, _____

Súper buenas noticias ¡Guau!

Esta nota lleva buenas noticias sobre _____.

Hoy él/ ella merece un gran abrazo por_____

_____

¡Que vivan las cosas buenas que suceden en la escuela!

Cordialmente, _____

Súper buenas noticias ¡Guau!

Esta nota lleva buenas noticias sobre _____.

Hoy él/ ella merece un gran abrazo por_____

_____

¡Que vivan las cosas buenas que suceden en la escuela!

Cordialmente, _____

 Name _____

☺ My Accomplishments ☺

We have been very busy in school.

Date: _____

Dear _____ ,

We have been working on _____

_____

_____ .

I want to tell you about my work on these things:

_____

_____

_____

_____

_____

_____

_____ .

I really enjoyed _____

because _____ .

Thanks for letting me share my work with you.

Love,

_____

 Nombre_____

Mis logros

Hemos estado muy ocupados en la escuela.

Fecha: _____

Querido/a_____ ,

Trabajamos en _____

_____

_____ .

Quiero contarte acerca de mi trabajo en estas cosas:

_____

_____

_____

_____

_____ .

Disfruté mucho _____

porque_____ .

Gracias por permitirme compartir mi trabajo contigo.

Con amor,

_____

Stop by or call me.

I want to tell you about

_____

_____

_____

_____

_____ .

Signed, _____

 -

Stop by or call me.

I want to tell you about

_____

_____

_____

_____

_____ .

Signed, _____

reproducible

Pase o llámeme.

Quiero contarle acerca de

_____

_____

_____

_____

_____ .

Firmado, _____

 -

Pase o llámeme.

Quiero contarle acerca de

_____

_____

_____

_____

_____ .

Firmado, _____

8. Self-Esteem

A student who does not have a favorable opinion of his own self worth is at a major disadvantage. It is important for each child to feel like a valuable member of the class. Highlighting each child for a day (or a week) helps him or her experience that sense of importance.

V.I.P. (Very Important Person)

This note lets parents know that their children are being highlighted in the classroom. It should be laminated, attached to a large manila envelope, and sent home so that the student and his or her parents can collect items to be brought in. Send the kit home on the Thursday or Friday before a child's V.I.P. week to allow time for collecting items. (WC)

Person of the Week

This form is to be filled out by the person of the week at school or at home. The completed form is mounted on construction paper and posted in the classroom. It should be displayed for the whole week in a prominent place. When the week is over, the form can be placed in the student's portfolio or added to a class book. (WC)

You're Invited

This note invites the V.I.P.'s parents to visit the classroom. Parents can bring in special treasures and memory items to share with the class. This is a good time for students to share pets, since the animals will have transportation to and from school and adult supervision while at school. Be sure to give parents plenty of advance notice so they can plan their schedules and locate appropriate items to share. If parents are not available, suggest that another relative come in their place. (WC)

It's a Celebration

This letter requests that parents write down a few thoughts about their children that can be read to the class on the children's birthdays or during their V.I.P. weeks. Be sure to send the form home with enough time for parents to fill it out and return it by the special date. (WC)

It's My Birthday

This form highlights a student's uniqueness. The birthday boy or girl can fill it out for his or her special day. It can be filled out either at school or at home. Once filled out, the form can be mounted on construction paper and displayed on the student's birthday.

My Treasure

Most students love to share treasured items with classmates. This form should be filled out and placed with the student's special item on display in the classroom. A picture of the treasure can be drawn in the corner box. (WC)

Dear _____ ,

Next week we will celebrate your child as our

Very Important Person.

Please place items in this envelope that you would like to have displayed
on the classroom bulletin board.
Include anything that is easy to display but not too precious to leave in the classroom.
These items will be returned to you when the week is over.

Sincerely, _____

 ✂ - ✂

Dear _____ ,

Next week we will celebrate your child as our

Very Important Person.

Please place items in this envelope that you would like to have displayed
on the classroom bulletin board.
Include anything that is easy to display but not too precious to leave in the classroom.
These items will be returned to you when the week is over.

Sincerely, _____

 **V.I.P.**

Estimado _____ ,

La semana que viene celebraremos a su niño/a como nuestra

Persona Muy Importante.

Por favor, ponga en este sobre artículos que quisiera mostrar en la cartelera de clase.
Incluya todo lo que sea fácil de mostrar, pero no demasiado valioso para dejar en el aula.
Estos objetos se le devolverán al terminar la semana.

Cordialmente, _____

 **V.I.P.**

Estimado _____ ,

La semana que viene celebraremos a su niño/a como nuestra

Persona Muy Importante.

Por favor, ponga en este sobre artículos que quisiera mostrar en la cartelera de clase.
Incluya todo lo que sea fácil de mostrar, pero no demasiado valioso para dejar en el aula.
Estos objetos se le devolverán al terminar la semana.

Cordialmente, _____

Person of the Week

Me! _____

I am _____ years old, and I am in the _____ grade.

My Favorites

Food	**Color**
Animal	**Thing to do**
My family	**Me as a grown-up**

PERSONA DE LA SEMANA

¡YO!_____

Tengo _____ años, y estoy en _____ grado.

Mis Preferidos

Comida	**Color**
Animal	**Algo para hacer**
Mi Familia	**Cuando sea grande**

You're Invited

For the week of_____,

we will be celebrating _____.

Dear Parents,

We would like you to come to our classroom for a visit. Please bring some special items or memories about _____ to share with us.

Please come on _____ at _____.

If this is not convenient, please call me at _____ and we'll reschedule.

We are looking forward to your visit.

Thanks,

_____

Están invitados

Para la semana de _____,

celebraremos_____.

Estimados padres/ encargados:

Nos gustaría que vinieran a visitarnos a nuestra aula. Por favor, traigan

algunos objetos especiales o recuerdos sobre _____

para compartir con nosotros.

Vengan el día_____ a las _____.

Si no les resulta conveniente, llámenme al_____y acordaremos otro momento.

No podemos ver la hora hasta su visita.

Muchas gracias,

_____

It's a
Celebration!

Dear Parent,

We will be celebrating _____.

In the space below, please write down a few things about your child for me to share with the class.

                    Thanks, _____

About _____

by _____

_____

_____

_____

_____

_____

¡Hay una celebración!

Estimado padre/ madre/ encargado:

Celebraremos _____.

En el espacio de abajo, por favor, escriba algunos datos sobre su niño/a para que yo los comparta con la clase.

      Gracias,_____

Acerca de_____

por_____

_____

_____

_____

_____

_____.

© Fearon Teacher Aids FE11050

It's My Birthday

Today is my special day!
Here's what I have to say!

My full name is _____.

I was born on _____.

My first word was _____.

My favorite toy was _____.

I have _____ brothers and _____ sisters.

I have _____ pets.

My pet's names are _____ and _____.

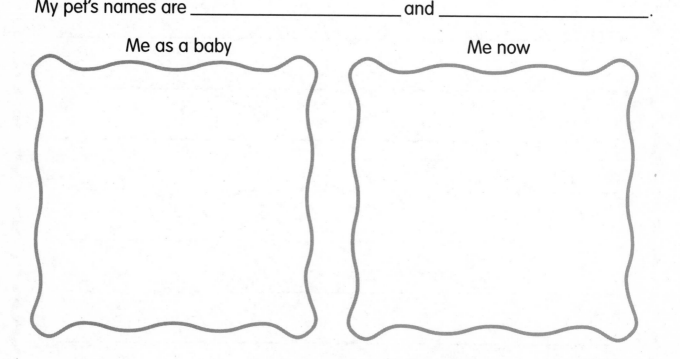

Me as a baby

Me now

106

Es mi cumpleaños

¡Hoy es un día especial para mí!
¡Esto es lo que tengo para decir!

Mi nombre completo es _____.

Nací el día_____.

Mi primera palabra fue _____.

Mi juguete preferido era _____.

Tengo _____ hermanos y _____ hermanas.

Tengo _____ mascotas.

Los nombres de mis mascotas son _____y_____.

Yo de bebé   Yo ahora

© Fearon Teacher Aids FE11050

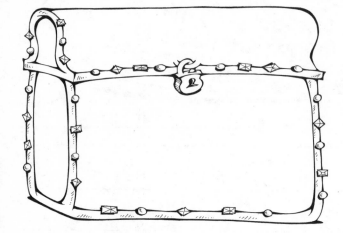

My Treasure

This belongs to

_____.

It is a

_____.

It is special because

_____

_____

_____.

I usually keep it

_____.

 -

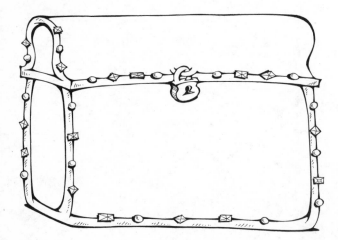

My Treasure

This belongs to

_____.

It is a

_____.

It is special because

_____

_____

_____.

I usually keep it

_____.

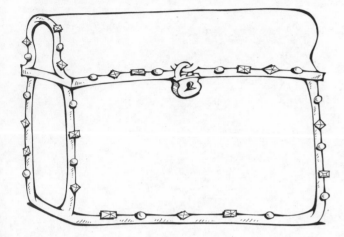

Mi tesoro

Esto le pertenece a

_____.

Es un/a

_____.

Es especial para mí porque

_____

_____

_____.

Lo suelo guardar

_____.

✂ --- ✂

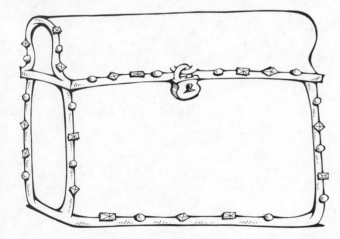

Mi tesoro

Esto le pertenece a

_____.

Es un/a

_____.

Es especial para mí porque

_____

_____

_____.

Lo suelo guardar

_____.

© Fearon Teacher Aids FE11050

9. End of the Year

As your year comes to an end, there will be many details to take care of. Keeping actively in touch with students' parents is essential to tying up all loose ends and will help your year end as gracefully as it began.

Classroom Cleanup

This note asks parents to look around at home for items that belong at school. Send it out several weeks before the end of the term, early enough for parents to have time to search. If necessary, specific items can be listed for each child. This note can also be used at other times during the year when you do a classroom cleanup. To use during the year, simply delete the words *for the end of the year* before copying. (*WC*)

Grade ____ in Review

This form itemizes subject areas mastered during the year and those needing review. The form helps parents know on which areas their children should work over the summer. (*I*)

Way to Go!

A happy way to send students off to the next grade. These can be given out during a class celebration or slipped into students' folders to be enjoyed at home. The form can be copied onto construction paper for a more festive look. (*WC*)

Read, Read, Read

This reminds parents of the importance of having their children read during summer vacation. Attach a list of recommended books. Parents often feel more comfortable searching out books that have been recommended by the teacher. (*WC*)

Packet of Summer Fun

This note can be attached to work suggested for the summer. Specific skills can be written on the line provided. Using this method, the form can be suited to each child's needs. If individualization is not desired, just write basic topics on the line before copying. (*WC*)

Classroom Cleanup

We're doing a classroom cleanup and we need your help!

Date: _____

Dear Parents,

We are cleaning up our classroom for the end of the year. Please look around your house for anything that might belong to school.

Specific items to look for include:

_____

_____

_____

_____

_____.

Thanks for your help!

_____

Limpieza del aula

¡Estamos haciendo una limpieza del aula y necesitamos su ayuda!

Fecha:_____

Estimados Padres/ Encargados:

Estamos limpiando el aula para el fin de año. Por favor, busquen en su casa cualquier cosa que pueda pertenecer a la escuela.

Los artículos específicos que pueden buscar incluyen:

_____

_____

_____

_____

_____.

¡Gracias por su ayuda!

_____

Grade _____ in Review

This year, _____ worked on many concepts. He/she seemed to fully understand the areas of

_____

_____

_____.

Some areas that were difficult for him/her were

_____

_____

_____.

Please review these areas over the summer:

_____

_____

_____.

Feel free to call if you need specific ideas to use in these areas.

Thanks for your support.

Sincerely, _____

Revisión de _____ grado

Este año, _____ trabajó sobre muchos conceptos. Él/ ella parece comprender totalmente las áreas de

_____

_____

_____ .

Algunas áreas que le resultaron difíciles fueron

_____

_____

_____ .

Por favor revea estas áreas durante el verano:

_____

_____

_____ .

Llame con confianza si necesita ideas específicas para usar en estas áreas.

Gracias por su apoyo.

Cordialmente, _____

First place award for

completing _____ grade!

 Good luck in _____ grade

Signed,

_____

✂ - ✂

First place award for

completing _____ grade!

Good luck in _____ grade

Signed,

_____

¡Primer premio por completar_____ grado!

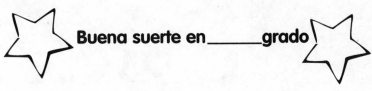

Buena suerte en_____grado

Firmado,

_____

¡Primer premio por completar_____ grado!

Buena suerte en_____ grado

Firmado,

_____

READ READ Read

Dear Parent,

I hope that you will encourage your child to read this summer.
The more you can read to him/her or have your child read to you,
the better.

Attached is a list of suggested books. These books are available
at the local library or bookstore. Some might be available at used
book stores.

**Enjoy a summer
of good reading.**

LEER LEER LEER

Estimado Padre/ Madre/ Encargado:

Espero que aliente a su niño/a a leer este verano. Cuanto más pueda leerle a su niño/a o hacer que él/ ella le lea a usted, mejor.

Adjuntamos una lista de libros sugeridos. Estos libros están disponibles en la biblioteca local o en las librerías. Algunos pueden encontrarse en librerías de libros usados.

**Disfrute un verano
de buena lectura.**

Packet of
Summer
Fun

Dear Parent,

Please help your child with these pages during this summer.

By working on _____

each week, your child will be off to a good start for next year.

Enjoy your summer!

Sincerely, _____

Packet of
Summer
Fun

Dear Parent,

Please help your child with these pages during this summer.

By working on _____

each week, your child will be off to a good start for next year.

Enjoy your summer!

Sincerely, _____

Paquete de
Diversión para el
verano

Estimado Padre/ Madre/ Encargado:

Por favor, ayude a su niño/a con estas páginas durante el verano. Al trabajar sobre

_____

cada semana, él/ ella estará listo/a para un buen comienzo el año entrante.

¡Disfrute el verano!

Cordialmente,_____

Paquete de
Diversión para el
verano

Estimado Padre/ Madre/ Encargado:

Por favor, ayude a su niño/a con estas páginas durante el verano. Al trabajar sobre

_____

cada semana, él/ ella estará listo/a para un buen comienzo el año entrante.

¡Disfrute el verano!

Cordialmente,_____